Sensory Smarts

also by Kathleen A. Chara and Paul J. Chara, Jr.

Allergy Busters
A Story for Children with Autism or Related Spectrum Disorders
Struggling with Allergies
Kathleen A. Chara and Paul J. Chara, Jr. with Karston J. Chara
Illustrated by J.M. Berns
ISBN 978 1 84310 782 8

of related interest

Sensory Perceptual Issues in Autism and Asperger Syndrome
Different Sensory Experiences – Different Perceptual Worlds
Olga Bogdashina
Foreword by Wendy Lawson
Foreword by Theo Peeters
ISBN 978 1 84310 166 6

Can I tell you about Asperger Syndrome?
A Guide for Friends and Family
Jude Welton
Illustrated by Jane Telford
Foreword by Elizabeth Newson
ISBN 978 1 84310 206 9

Freaks, Geeks and Asperger Syndrome
A User Guide to Adolescence
Luke Jackson
Foreword by Tony Attwood
ISBN 978 1 84310 098 0

Sensory Smarts

A Book for Kids with ADHD or Autism Spectrum Disorders Struggling with Sensory Integration Problems

**Kathleen A. Chara and Paul J. Chara, Jr.
with Christian P. Chara**

Illustrated by J.M. Berns

Jessica Kingsley Publishers
London and Philadelphia

First published in 2004
by Jessica Kingsley Publishers
116 Pentonville Road
London N1 9JB, UK
and
400 Market Street, Suite 400
Philadelphia, PA 19106, USA

www.jkp.com

Library of Congress Cataloging in Publication Data
Chara, Kathleen A. (Kathleen Ann), 1965-
     Sensory smarts : a book for kids with ADHD or autism spectrum disorders struggling with sensory integration problems / Kathleen A. Chara, Paul J. Chara, Jr. and Christian P. Chara ; illustrated by J.M. Berns.
          p. cm.
     Includes bibliographical references.
     ISBN 1-84310-783-X (pbk.)
     1. Chara, Christian P. (Christian Paul), 1991---Mental health. 2. Attention-deficit-disordered children--Biography 3. Hyperactive children--Behavior modification--Juvenile literature. 4. Senses and sensation in children--Juvenile literature. I. Chara, Paul J. (Paul John), 1953- II. Berns, J. M. (Jane M.) III. Title.
     RJ506.H9C473 2004
     618.92'8589--dc22

                                                                2004010962

British Library Cataloguing in Publication Data
A CIP catalogue record for this book is available from the British Library

ISBN 978 1 84310 783 5

Contents

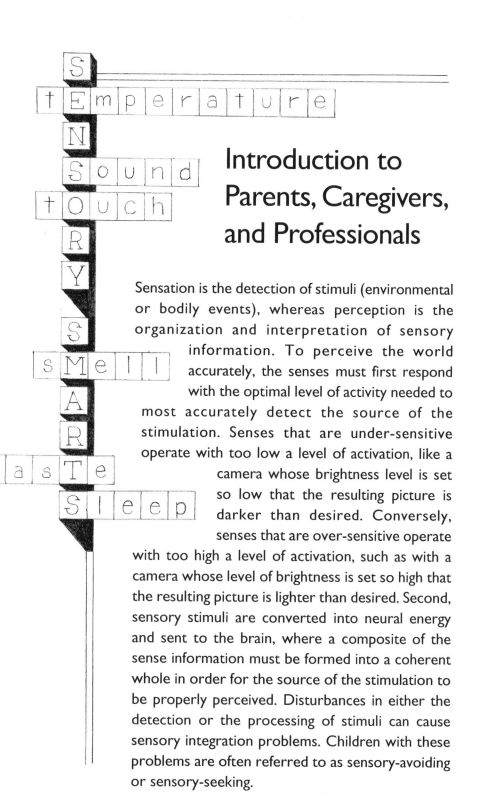

Introduction to Parents, Caregivers, and Professionals

Sensation is the detection of stimuli (environmental or bodily events), whereas perception is the organization and interpretation of sensory information. To perceive the world accurately, the senses must first respond with the optimal level of activity needed to most accurately detect the source of the stimulation. Senses that are under-sensitive operate with too low a level of activation, like a camera whose brightness level is set so low that the resulting picture is darker than desired. Conversely, senses that are over-sensitive operate with too high a level of activation, such as with a camera whose level of brightness is set so high that the resulting picture is lighter than desired. Second, sensory stimuli are converted into neural energy and sent to the brain, where a composite of the sense information must be formed into a coherent whole in order for the source of the stimulation to be properly perceived. Disturbances in either the detection or the processing of stimuli can cause sensory integration problems. Children with these problems are often referred to as sensory-avoiding or sensory-seeking.

Children with sensory integration problems react differently from most other children. Sensory-avoiders are often described with such terms as avoiding, overactive, emotional, unstable, and sensory inappropriate. Sensory-seekers are often described as intrusive and impulsive, as well as overactive, emotional, and unstable. It is important to note that some children may be primarily sensory-avoiding, others may be primarily sensory-seeking, and still others may be a combination of both types.

Some children with sensory integration problems may be picky and isolate themselves, while others may be controlling and aggressive. Many of their self-care skills are also disrupted. The symptoms may be mild, moderate, or severe and are often mistaken for signs of other disorders, attention deficit hyperactivity disorder (ADHD) being a common misdiagnosis. Most children on the autism spectrum also have sensory integration problems; in fact, common physiological disturbances may underlie both disorders. Furthermore, many children with sensory issues experience developmental delays.

Sensory integration problems are still not well understood among parents, teachers, and physicians. As a result, our struggle to have our then almost five-year-old son Christian properly diagnosed was difficult at best. We were told many inaccurate things about him: "He is just shy", "He's so disobedient", "What a hyperactive child he is", "Your expectations for him are too high." When we talked to professionals about his developmental issues we were told things like: "He is just a boy", "Einstein had problems too", "He will grow out of it." Unfortunately for Christian, he was our first child so we lacked the knowledge and experience to properly deal with his condition.

Something that really got our attention and started us on the road to making genuine progress in helping Christian was a story that we read about a young child fighting against a haircut. Kathleen, in particular, identified with the struggling barber and recalled the high levels of frustration caused to her and our son when she would cut his hair. (Going to the barber was out of the question!) The author of that story, however, encouraged readers to "pity the child, not the barber." Those words made us stop and think and reframe the problem. Somehow, Christian's struggle had gotten lost in our own frustration. We felt so bad about getting upset with him without putting ourselves in his shoes. We needed to understand Christian's perspective and the nature of his condition, and to forgive ourselves, in order to overcome a situation that was going to require a lot of work on everyone's part.

It is our sincere hope that telling our story or, better put, Christian's story, will help other struggling families in some small way. For further assistance, we have included a rating scale for symptoms of sensory integration for both sensory-avoiders and sensory-seekers at the back of this book, along with a list of helpful resources. However, none of the pages in this book should be considered medical advice. If you suspect that your child has sensory issues, we suggest that you consult with a certified occupational therapist with specialized training in sensory integration.

Our hearts are with you and your children!

Sensory Smarts

My name is Christian and I am 12 years old. When I was five years old, my parents learned that I had sensory integration problems. What this means is that my body was not feeling, smelling, tasting, hearing, seeing, or developing like it should. I didn't know others were different from me and others didn't know I was different from them. Maybe you have sensory issues too. If you do, remember that you are not the only kid who has this problem. Lots of kids have sensory issues—we are not the only ones! When kids have problems with sensory issues, things like **touch**, **sound**, **taste**, **smell**, **temperature**, **interactions with others**, **activity/energy level**, and **sleeping** seem different to us than to kids who don't have sensory problems. Some kids are called **sensory-avoiders**, which means that they avoid or dislike many sensations, such as loud sounds or certain touches. Other kids are **sensory-seekers**, which means that they tend to seek out a lot of sensations—they like loud noises and want to touch everything around them. I was mainly a sensory-avoider, but in some ways I was also a sensory-seeker. Maybe you are just learning about all of this and are just beginning therapy to help you and your family work on these things. Let me tell you the story of my life with sensory issues and then about going to therapy for help! Remember, I got help and so can you!!

I was my parents' first child and was born on June 9, 1991. Early in my mom's pregnancy, she had an infection and ran a fever. Although I was born on time, it was a long, difficult delivery. My dad thought that it was so long there would have been enough time to have another child! The cord that connected me to my mom so I could eat before I was born was wrapped around my neck. My mom said she learned later that birth problems and infections in pregnancy are common with children with sensory integration problems. After I came home from the hospital, I continued to have a hard time. I cried all the time. Have your parents told you things about you that concerned them when you were a baby?

Kids like us may have trouble **sleeping**. When I was a baby, I had difficulty sleeping and really only napped a few times a day. My dad said once he got up with me 22 times before 3:00 in the morning and then stopped counting! I think that story is funny (although I don't think my dad did at the time!). Other kids find the sheets in their bed or certain types of pajamas to be uncomfortable. Even dim lights or tiny noises at night-time can be big problems. I found out that sleeping on flannel sheets or warming my pajamas in the dryer before bedtime helped me not be such a restless sleeper. Sensory-seekers may need more rest and have to have an extra nap during the day! After I started sleeping through the night, I also took two- to three-hour naps in the day-time until I was seven years old. I guess I was just making up for lost sleep!

Some kids have problems with the sense of **taste**, which can affect what and how we eat. My mom had a hard time breastfeeding me when I was a baby, so I went on a special formula (easier to digest) and had medication (to reduce gas) after each feeding. Most kids like us continue to be real picky eaters when we get older. A lot of kids like us think that vegetables and foods with cheese taste HORRIBLE. Others though, say that strongly spiced foods are their favorites! Go figure. Learning how to eat properly with eating utensils was very hard for me and most people thought I was the messiest eater in the world. My dad thought I was one of the great mysteries of the universe. He'd sometimes say,

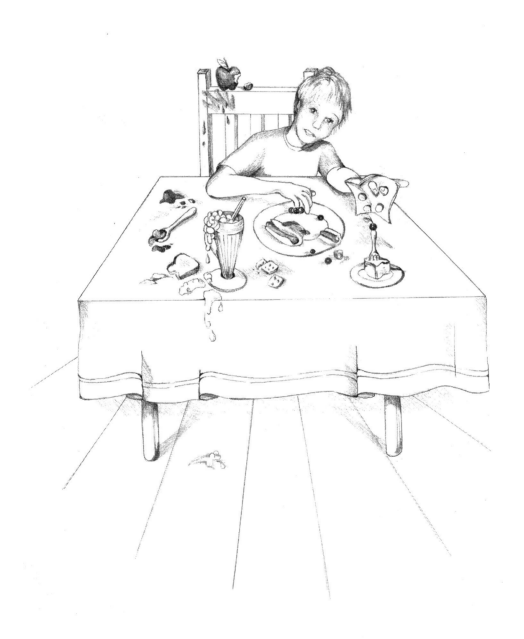

"How could a kid eat so little, yet make such a big mess?" Other things like pouring, cutting, and sitting still at the table made mealtimes even harder. Although I wouldn't eat most foods, I loved to chew on things like pencils, clothes, and toys. Maybe my parents should've made my food look like toys!

Well, I bet I drove my parents crazy because I disliked most foods, especially new foods or foods with different textures to them. But I wasn't trying to drive them nuts— these sensory issues were driving *me* nuts!! How about you—do you have trouble with certain foods? Are there many foods that bother you?

To make matters worse, many kids with sensory issues also have food allergies. One problem on top of another! Then, of course, after mealtimes came brushing teeth—I really hated this!! Some kids cannot take the taste of certain toothpastes. If you dislike the taste of your toothpaste, you should try several different brands of toothpaste—most kids find at least one that they can tolerate. My big problem was that I hated the feeling of brushing my teeth. My parents thought that I was going to become the only kid in town with yellow hair AND yellow teeth! Yuk! Some kids have found the electrical toothbrush to be helpful and extra fun (it is great for sensory-seekers too!).

Sometimes kids with sensory issues can have problems with **touch** and **temperature**. When I was a baby, baths were also difficult until my parents started bathing me in cool water. Tags in clothes can bug lots of kids like you and me. My parents always cut the tags out of my clothes because they bothered me. I was also hot all the time and disliked hats, sweaters, and zipping winter coats. Other kids are just the opposite and are cold all the time. They love to wear lots of clothing and keep hats and blankets on them—even in summer! Having my face washed or anything done to my hair was also very stressful to my family and me. Sensory-seekers go the opposite way with touch, wanting to touch everything. This includes such stuff as sucking their thumbs after five years of age, frequently picking at their scabs, or being excessively ticklish. My dad says that I'm the only person he knows that has ticklish elbows. Guess I just have extra funny bones! How about you—what sort of things with touch or temperature bother you? I found out that when people just let me decide whether or not something bothers me, life is easier for everyone.

Sounds can be hard for kids like us to handle too! My mom said that although I was a very loud child (sensory-seeker), I hated loud noises from other people or other things (sensory-avoider). Sweepers seemed to especially bother me when I was younger, so one parent would vacuum while the other left the house with me. It is common for kids with sensory issues to hum a lot or avoid loud sounds like fireworks or fire drills. Others seem not to notice certain sounds, like their own names being called (I must admit that this comes in handy at chore-time!). If fire

drills bother you, have the school tell your parents what days the school will practice these drills so you can prepare. Special helpers, such as occupational therapists, teachers, or parents, can give many kids like us ideas to help us figure out what is bothering us. Some kids find it helpful to find a quiet, uncluttered space where they can relax (such as under a table or a blanket) and try to figure out what sensory issues are troubling them and how they can deal with it.

Another thing that I found helpful, after I was able to figure out what sensory issues were bothering me, was to have a list of my favorite coping activities. I found these activities helped keep me focused, by either calming me down or helping me stay alert, depending on the situation. A lot of these activities are listed in the back of this book. I hope they work for you!

When I grew older I found it helpful to have my special helpers put my loudness on a number line. For example, on a number line, ten could stand for screaming, five could be a talking voice you would use indoors (my parents call this an "inside voice"), and one could be a faint whisper. Sometimes I would think that I was talking at a five but my parents would say, "Christian, you are talking at a seven, please lower your voice to a five." This activity is fun because I would draw a number line and practice talking at all the number levels of loudness.

Most parents of kids like us are often worried, confused, and very tired. Life can be difficult for all of us, but, when I was little, the doctors said my problems were just from colic and they told my parents not to worry. Things did get better for me for a while. I started sleeping through the night at two and a half years, so my parents thought my troubles

might soon be over. But new problems soon began. For kids like us who have problems with sensory issues, it can be hard to be around other people. The problems in interacting with others are sometimes referred to as **social problems**. My dad said I would not coo with others as a baby but would only look straight ahead like a frozen soldier. I laugh a lot about that story! I am sure your parents have some funny stories about you too! I often disliked going outside, even to play. The brightness of the sun would bother me and I wanted to avoid people, especially people who talked to me or touched me. I hated touch—it usually hurt. I also found it hard to sit still, and I always wanted to prop my feet up on chairs. This made going to places such as school or church even harder.

Kids like us often dislike looking into people's eyes when we speak to them, so we hear grown-ups say a lot, "Look in my eyes when you talk to me." At first, I would look away, but then I began to look right below their eyes. Slowly, I began to look into people's eyes…well, just a little bit at first! I didn't always understand what the look on people's faces really meant like other kids my age did, so I had my parents help me with that too! It all helps, so listen to what your parents tell you. It is usually easiest to practice eye contact with a conversation or activity that you really enjoy. I loved to watch my dad's electric trains go round and round when I was little. Now I love to play sports—keep your eye on the ball, my dad always says! My mom says that normal eye contact between two people occurs only 30 percent to 60 percent of the time. I used to think that 30 percent was way too much, but now even 31 percent doesn't bother me (ha ha!).

Another thing that kids like us may have problems with are certain **smells**. There are some smells that I just cannot take. For example, I hate the smell of peanut butter. Unfortunately, my brother Karston loves the stuff. Sometimes he will open up a jar of peanut butter and chase me around the house with it if I get him angry. I also hate the smell of bleach, especially when my dad overdoes it cleaning the bathroom! Common smells other kids have problems with are glue, cleaning supplies, or certain foods. Some people do not understand that we smell things differently and that it can make us really sick or distracted. It is important to teach this to the important people in our lives so that they can make good choices too! I once told a teacher I would throw up if I had to work with certain chemicals, but she said, "You are doing it anyways!" My parents decided that they needed to talk to other grown-ups BEFORE they spend time with me (or I throw up on them!). This has worked great—I suggest your parents do the same.

What is interesting about smells is that almost all kids with sensory integration problems—whether sensory-avoiders or sensory-seekers—seem to have strong reactions to smells. My dad says that this might be because the sense of smell has the most immediate connection to the brain. So, I guess that means that for us the bad smells are even worse and the good smells are even better. I think that sensory-seekers must really need to smell good smells. In fact, I know one girl whose mom would place a small amount of lavender oil on her wrists so that when she was at school she could have something good to smell!

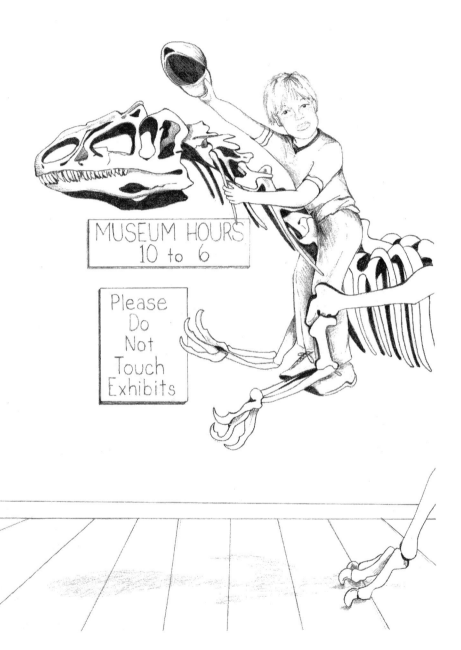

Kids' **activity or energy levels** can also be affected by sensory issues. We found out that the number line used for voice loudness could be used in a similar way for activity level. When I was a little older, I became very active and difficult to control in public. My mom thought I was hyperactive and needed medicine. My parents talked about medicine and decided against it, so we all struggled on. Lots of kids are on medicine though and, if you are, it is important to take your medicine and vitamins. I take my vitamins EVERY DAY—even though sometimes they are a big pain—you should too! I never told my parents that I had all these problems and at first they didn't ask many questions. I was born this way—I didn't know life could be different. How about you—do you think everyone feels, thinks, acts, or hears like you? I sure was surprised to learn not all people have this problem. It is nice to know that some problems can be fixed.

Other times kids like us may have **handwriting** problems. When I was three and a half years old, my mom noticed I didn't color like the other kids. She also noticed that I seemed physically weaker than most kids my age. Many kids have a hard time learning to write or have very messy handwriting. My handwriting was so bad that my dad thought that I was destined to become a physician! Homework can be a frustrating time for everyone, but special helpers can help your parents try to find the right tools for you! I had a special chair at home and one at school that was made especially for me. I also used grippers on my pencils, which helped with the pain when I had to do a lot of writing. If handwriting is hard for you to do too, there is a fun and easy program, *Handwriting Without Tears*, listed in the 'Helpful Organizations' section of this book.

Another thing kids like us may have some problems with is **coordination**. Some kids are clumsy, fall a lot, or are accident-prone. Sometimes kids step on others' feet, even when they don't really mean to. On many days, dressing was a hard part of the day for me. My mom said I would not snap my pants but rather would just suck in my stomach and pull them on without unsnapping them. I would also never untie my shoes—instead I would just slip them on and off. I still dislike tying shoes. That's why I think that buying shoes with Velcro® until you master tying is a great option!! I think Velcro® is the greatest invention since the sandwich! As a result of these sensory issues, kids like us sometimes find playing some sports really difficult. I really enjoy sports now, though, so keep trying.

Because of all the problems I was having when I was younger, my parents decided to have some tests done with me to see if I was okay. The tests said everything was okay, but the lady doing the tests said that I had to "just learn to listen to other adults." My mom knew I needed help, but she said she couldn't find anyone to listen. I'm sure that lots of parents ask for help from lots of different kinds of people before finding out what the problems really are. Did your parents ask for help but were told the wrong information too?

My mom says that she didn't know how much all these things bothered me or that they were so hard for me to do. She says she is sorry now. She thought I was fighting to not do an activity like have my hair cut or combed, but now she knows I was fighting to stop the feelings from these different sensory activities. Parenting kids like us is a hard job sometimes, but remember your mom and dad love you even if you're not perfect!

My mom said she made tons of mistakes before she knew I had problems. "Sorry" is an important word to learn to say in families like ours. Also, if something is bothering you, tell your parents. I have found that if I use kind words they tend to listen better—I suggest you try kind words too!

Shortly before I started kindergarten, my mom decided to go through our phone book to find someone who might help with my problems. My coloring had not gotten better and I still had a very hard time being around other people and lots of things bothered me like clothing and heat.

My mom called a lady named Janet who is a physical therapist. She did some more tests…different tests. Did you have tons of tests too? Remember, tests are okay to have done because they will help your family and therapists help you even more!

It was a good thing that she did those tests because I found out that I had some problems, some rather big problems. Janet told my parents that I had sensory integration problems. She also told them that I had fine and gross motor delays. This meant that I really wasn't as strong as the other kids were. I found out that my neck and stomach muscles were similar to most two-year-olds, even though I was five years old. My parents then tried to learn as much as they could about sensory issues to help me even more.

I went to see my physical therapist every week for a very long time. She was nice and really fun. Most kids with problems like mine see a different special helper called an occupational therapist. My parents say that most insurance companies only pay for occupational therapy for sensory issues. What are the names of your special helpers? It sure is great to have lots of people who care about kids like us, isn't it?

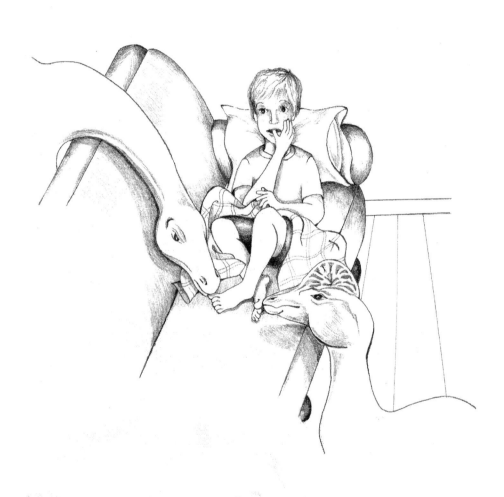

After a lot of testing, one thing my therapist had me do (with the help of my family) was to start on a brushing program, which means my parents brushed my arms, legs, back, hands, and feet with a special brush. This brush is really different from a hairbrush and it was supposed to help my body learn to feel things like other kids do instead of how I did. I hated the brushing at first, though. It felt like dinosaurs nibbling at my skin! When my mom said that the brushing felt good to her body, I could hardly believe it. And here's something strange: most sensory-seekers LOVE to be brushed. Weird! But remember there are lots of different ways to help our bodies. You and your therapist can come up with some neat ideas to help your body too—not all kids need the same stuff.

The brushing program was a real pain! My body was brushed every one and a half hours for six weeks. It was the longest six weeks of my life. (Mom agrees!) I was supposed to use a different brush for my mouth, but I kept biting through it (ha ha!). This brush was to help me stop chewing on everything. Mom said that once she bought me a brand new sweatshirt for school and I bit a large hole in it on the first day. I would bite through this special mouth brush so my parents bought me several teething rings for babies even though I was five years old. I used them for several years to help me not chew on my fingers, clothes, or toys. My parents also thought that I was not as loud when I used them. I'm not sure how it all works, but it did help! I sometimes did not want to do all this hard work, but remember, therapy can help YOU and ME a lot!

Janet, my therapist, gave my family and me many fun activities to do at home to help my body even more. You and your therapist can do the same. Some activities were extra fun, like playing with bubbles, writing on carpet with chalk, and using beads in play dough. Although they were fun, it was hard work too!

To help me get even stronger, Janet and I worked and worked. I would do special exercises with her and at home. Janet had lots of fun games for us to do together. Sometimes I would sit or lay across balls to play a game like catch. My brother, Karston, sometimes liked to join in on the fun! I would even help Janet move the heavy mats, which was really hard work. My favorite thing to do was being wrapped up in a blanket while Janet and Mom would swing me! I bet you would love these swings too! Do you have a favorite swing at home or at therapy?

I would play on other types of swings too when I went to therapy! Sometimes I would have to swing on my stomach— that was really hard for me. All these activities at home and in therapy helped my body get stronger and feel things more like other kids.

Other times I would get very tired and wish I didn't have to do all of these exercises. I'm glad now that I did. It doesn't hurt so much to do all the things that I want to do. One thing that I found helped me not grumble about doing all those activities at home was to have a sticker chart. Every day, when I did my activities with Mom or Dad, I would get a sticker! After so many stickers, I would get a treat or a small prize, such as an allergy-free dessert, extra TV time, or reading a special book. I have included a reward chart on page 66 that you can cut out or copy if you and your family like this idea. Remember, all families are different and that's okay.

I have learned a lot about sensory issues since I began therapy. I thought I would tell you about some helpful hints in case you could use some extra help too. I call these helpful hints **Sensory Keys**. You and I can both use these Sensory Keys to help us even more. Kids who use these Sensory Keys are **Sensory Smart**! I sure am glad I became Sensory Smart. Would you like to be Sensory Smart too? To be Sensory Smart, kids need to follow the four Sensory Keys so that they can take control of their sensory issues and start having more fun in life. Here are the four Sensory Keys. I sure do hope you use them. If you do, then you will be Sensory Smart too! Well, let's get smart!

Sensory Key #1

LEARN about sensory issues and TEACH others about them.

People do not understand that we experience the world differently from them until we teach them about sensory issues. Can you list the sensory issues that bother you most? Knowing how you react to certain sensations and having fun ideas to help deal with these sensations can help you enjoy life more at home and school!! Remember to ask Mom, Dad, and other important people in your life about what they think bothers you too. See if you can complete this sentence:

"I am most bothered by _____, _____, and _____."

"I have found _____, _____, and _____ to help me with these issues."

(You don't have to fill in all the blanks.)

Sensory Key #2

WORK HARD in therapy and complete your home exercises/activities.

This key is important because if you don't do anything about your sensory problems, then you will probably never overcome those problems. Kids who are Sensory Smart work hard in therapy even if they are tired or want to do something else. Sensory Smart kids promise,

"I, _____ (your name), will work my hardest on sensory issues at home and therapy."

Sensory Key #3

Sensory Smart kids TELL others when sensory PROBLEMS occur.

Most of the time people don't know what's really bothering you unless you tell them. If you cannot find the words to say, but know something is bothering you, try using code words, such as CODE RED. Try this sample statement,

"The _____ (sensation)
of _____ (object or situation)
is bothering me, may I do or have something else?"

If you don't know what is bothering you, but you know that something is bothering you, just tell other people, "Something is bothering me!" Then ask them to help you figure out what the problem is. It is often helpful to go to a quiet place to sort this out. Remember, people are more likely to help you and be nicer to you if you use kind, gentle words.

Sensory Key #4

Sensory Smart kids are ALERT and PLAN AHEAD.

We think ahead if sensory issues could be a problem at a place where we are going, such as a museum, friend's house, or our favorite camp. And we are alert to what our reactions are likely to be in these places. We ask questions about activities and places BEFORE we go there. Special helpers have many useful ideas to help with sensory issues, like doing calming or alerting activities before visiting a museum. Try to fill in this statement:

"I will do _____ (name of coping activity) to help me with sensory problems before I go to _____."

Do you want to use these four Sensory Keys? Well, if so, then, CONGRATULATIONS!! You are now Sensory Smart too! Lots of kids are getting help by following these four simple Sensory Keys. I made a certificate (in the back of this book on page 76) to cut out or copy for all those who follow these four Sensory Keys and become Sensory Smart too! I sure do hope you join this group of Sensory Smart kids!

It has been several years since I began physical therapy. Many things have gotten better. Things can get better for you and your family too! Learning how to cut my food, tie my shoes, and button my clothes were very hard for me. It's okay if these things are hard for you too. My writing is still difficult at times so I am learning to type on the computer. I still see an occupational therapist called Bryn. I remember to follow Sensory Key #2 by working really hard to help me even more. Remember, don't give up—keep trying! It took a long, long time and lots of work but now I can do all those hard things without help.

Although I am not as strong as other kids my age, I'm much stronger now. I may never be like children who don't have sensory integration problems, but I'm just like them in many ways. Remember, it is alright just to be us.

Now I am almost a teenager and I love to have fun with my friends, ride my bike, collect sports cards, and play lots of different sports. My dad thinks that I am getting very good at basketball, especially when I swish a 3-pointer! I also like to do fun things with my family! My parents say that I am a big help with my brothers, Karston and Kristof, and my baby sister, Kristiana. I enjoy carrying my sister around—I never thought when I was younger I would be strong enough to do that!

This has been a long journey for my family and me, so I decided to write a book to let other families learn about sensory integration problems and to let kids like us know that things can get better. Keep working hard in therapy, and keep using your kind words and life can get easier for EVERYONE. Remember, Sensory Smart kids learn about their sensory issues, work hard in therapy, and complete their home activities. We use kind words to tell others when sensory issues bother us, and we are alert to potential sensory issues and plan ahead. Remember, you and your family can also make up code words to help let others know when sensory issues bother you. My family got help and so can yours!!

Your friend,

Christian

Christian, aka Sensory Smart

Sensitivity Scale

Directions: Circle the number on the rating scale to the left of each category that best describes your child. Examples of possible problems are listed for each category. Then add the numbers in each column to get subtotals. Combine the subtotals for A and B to get the *under-sensitive* score. Combining the D and E subtotals will result in the *over-sensitive* score.

The greater the departures from zero for the under-sensitive or over-sensitive scores, the greater the likelihood of sensory intergration problems.

	Very under-sensitive	Under-sensitive	Normal	Over-sensitive	Very over-sensitive
Rating Scale:	−2	−1	0	1	2

A	B	C	D	E	
−2	−1	0	1	2	*Light touch*: difficulties with gentle touching of face, body, and hair, writing, clothing or hair-cutting/brushing
−2	−1	0	1	2	*Pressure*: difficulties with hugging, firm grasping, rough play or wrestling
−2	−1	0	1	2	*Hot temperatures*: difficulties with bathing, inside or outside temperatures or clothing (removing?)
−2	−1	0	1	2	*Cold temperatures*: difficulties with bathing, inside or outside temperatures or clothing (excessive?)
−2	−1	0	1	2	*Pain*: hurts/injuries exaggerated or ignored; response poorly connected with stimulus
−2	−1	0	1	2	*Tickling*: highly responsive or minimal/absent response to tickling

A	B	C	D	E	
−2	−1	0	1	2	Vestibular stimulation (sense of balance): easily loses balance; excessive love or fear of spinning, turning, rolling (slides, swings, ramps, etc.); coordination difficulties
−2	−1	0	1	2	*Proprioception (body position awareness)*: abnormal awareness of body in space; too high or low activity level; sloppiness; clumsiness; resistance to new movements
−2	−1	0	1	2	*Audition*: difficulty with loudness; pitch (tone of sound) discrimination abnormalities; poor listening ability; improper regulation of voice loudness
−2	−1	0	1	2	*Vision*: difficulty with brightness (or darkness); poor eye contact; staring; reading problems; focus on repetitive sights (e.g., fans)
−2	−1	0	1	2	*Gustation*: finicky about food taste or texture; abnormal reaction to different tastes; chewing non-edibles; improperly chews food

Subtotals: A   B   D   E

___ ___ ___ ___

Under-sensitive score: A + B = ___

Over-sensitive score: D + E = ___

Note: We have not determined through research absolute cutoff scores. Scores beyond 11 are likely indicative of sensory problems.

Sensory Smarts Reward System

Guidelines for developing an effective reward system

The word reward is basically synonymous with the psychological term re-inforcement. Psychologists define reinforcement as any stimulus (an event or object) that increases the likelihood of a particular behavior. A reward can be a powerful tool for increasing the frequency of desirable behaviors. However, a century of psychological research has demonstrated that the effectiveness of using a reward system is greatly affected by how it is set up and how it is implemented. To help you maximize the effectiveness of your reward system, we offer the following guidelines, organized around three basic steps.

1. Identify the behaviors you want to change.

2. Determine what to use as a reward.

3. Aim for long-term success.

Step 1: Identify the behaviors you want to change

A. DETERMINE THE IMPORTANCE OF BEHAVIORS
Rank behaviors in order from most important (e.g., taking medication) to least important (e.g., wiping nose on sleeve).

B. DETERMINE THE EASE OF CHANGING BEHAVIORS
Rank behaviors in order from easiest for the child to change (e.g., taking vitamins) to hardest for the child to change (e.g., refusing an offer of a desirable food that is also an allergy trigger).

C. DETERMINE FREQUENCY OF BEHAVIORS
Rank behaviors in order from most frequent (e.g., complains a lot) to least frequent (e.g., rarely eats fruit).

Step 2: Determine what to use as a reward

A. TWO BASIC WAYS OF REWARDING BEHAVIOR

1. *Reward training.* If the child acceptably performs a desired behavior, a reward is given.

2. *Omission training.* If the child stops (or decreases to an acceptable level) an undesired behavior, a reward is given.

B. WHAT MAKES A GOOD REWARD?

1. *The matching principle.* The frequency of behavior will be affected by how much children value a particular reward. A reward that has little value to children will have little impact in changing their behavior. Ask the child to give you examples of what he or she thinks is a good reward. Then, within reasonable limits, negotiate with the child what the reward(s) will be.

2. *Salience.* Children will change their behavior to get a reward that has a high value to them. However, if the value is too high, once the reward is stopped or greatly lessened, the behavior changed by the reward will revert back to its pre-reward frequency. If the value of the reward is not too high, then even if the reward is stopped or greatly lessened the rewarded behavior is likely to maintain its rewarded frequency and not revert to its pre-reward rate of occurrence. For example, one child is given 20 gold coins for every book that is read, whereas another child is given only one small silver coin for each book that is read. The monetary rewards are then terminated for each child. The child rewarded with the 20 gold coins will most likely greatly decrease the time spent reading books or stop reading. However, the child given the smaller reward is likely to continue reading at the rate that was rewarded. Simply put, rewards that are too valuable lower the probability that a child will continue a behavior—after the reward for it is removed—for its own sake.

3. *The Premack principle*. Anything that a child does frequently can be used to reward something that the child does infrequently. For example, J.J. loves to watch television but hates to eat vegetables. J.J. is then put on a reward schedule where every time a certain amount of veggies are eaten, a certain amount of television viewing is gained. In other words, viewing television is made to be dependent on eating veggies.

4. *The token economy*. A token is something that is used to represent a reward. In a token economy, children earn tokens that are eventually redeemed for monetary rewards or other desirable activities/objects. For example, a plus (+) is used to represent a certain amount of money. A child is then told that plusses will be given for specific behaviors that the child performs. At the end of a specified time the plusses are counted and then exchanged for money. Most token economies include "reverse rewards" which can decrease the amount of tokens earned. Thus, good behaviors earn plusses and bad behaviors earn minuses, which reduce the number of plusses. Using "reverse rewards" provides consequences for undesirable behaviors and can increase the incentive for the child to perform desired behaviors—the child works extra hard to make up for the loss of plusses. However, if too many minuses are given, a child may lose the incentive to stick with the reward system. A token economy can provide a sense of immediate reward for the child (making the reward more effective) while delaying the administration of the actual reward (who wants to carry around a bag of coins in order to reward the child every time an acceptable behavior is performed?). Many children prefer stickers instead of plusses. Another approach is to have different levels of achievement: red = 1 reward; yellow = 2 rewards; green = 3 rewards; blue = 4 rewards.

Step 3: Aim for long-term success

A. START SMALL

1. Begin rewarding behaviors that are easiest and less important to change (see Step 1, A and B).

2. Begin using small amounts of rewards for these initial behaviors.

B. SHAPING

1. Gradually work in more difficult behaviors to change (see Step 1, A and C.).

2. Gradually increase the amount of rewards used: the more difficult and/or more important the behavior, the greater the amount of reward used to modify it (but keep in mind Step 2, B2).

C. KEYS TO LONG-TERM SUCCESS

1. *Consistency.* Once a reward system is begun, stick to it! If a day or more is missed, don't despair; just get back to the system. Keep in mind that the greater the consistency in using the reward system, the greater the likelihood of long-term success in developing positive behaviors.

2. *Attitude.* Make the reward system fun for the child! Deemphasize the failures and accentuate the successes. Give the child frequent feedback about how successful she or he has been, and encourage the child toward future successes.

3. *Frequency.* The more often and longer you use the reward system, the greater the likelihood that the rewarded behaviors will be permanently changed for the better! The reward system is helping children learn constructive habits, habits that are likely to be continued throughout their lives—even after the reward system is no longer used.

Suggested goals are given in the chart below. The second chart is blank for you to fill in yourself.

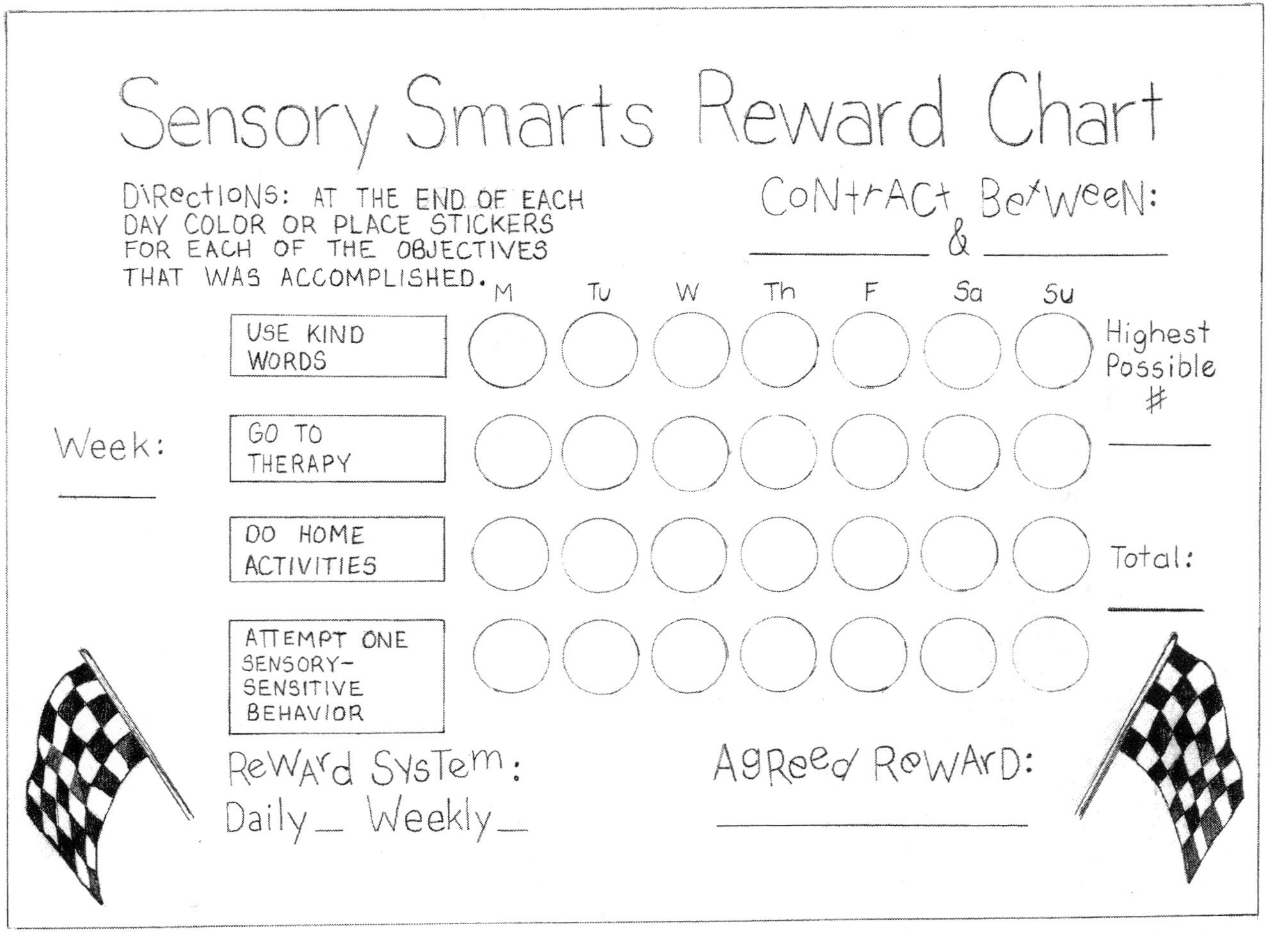

Sensory Smarts Reward Chart

CoNtrAct BetweeN:

_____ & _____

DiRectioNs: At the END of EACH DAY COLOR OR PLACE STICKERS FOR EACH OF THE OBJECTIVES THAT WAS ACCOMPLISHED.

Week: _____

	M	Tu	W	Th	F	Sa	Su	Highest Possible #
USE KIND WORDS	◯	◯	◯	◯	◯	◯	◯	_____
GO TO THERAPY	◯	◯	◯	◯	◯	◯	◯	
DO HOME ACTIVITIES	◯	◯	◯	◯	◯	◯	◯	Total:
ATTEMPT ONE SENSORY-SENSITIVE BEHAVIOR	◯	◯	◯	◯	◯	◯	◯	_____

RewArd SysteM: Daily__ Weekly__

AgReed RewArd: _____

Sensory Smarts Reward Chart

ContRact Between:
&
_____ _____

Directions: At the end of each
day color or place stickers
for each of the objectives
that was accomplished.

Week: _____

	M	Tu	W	Th	F	Sa	Su	Highest Possible #
	○	○	○	○	○	○	○	_____
	○	○	○	○	○	○	○	_____
	○	○	○	○	○	○	○	_____
	○	○	○	○	○	○	○	Total: _____

Reward System:
Daily __ Weekly __

Agreed Reward:
_____

s e l f - s o o t h i n g

S
E
E
K
I
N
G

t
a
c
t
i
l
e

"A calming technique."

l i g h t   s m e l l s

w
i
n
d

A
V
O
I
D
I
N
G

"Sensory Overload!"

PHYSICAL **THERAPY**

trunk muscles

"This is hard work!"

"Therapy is hard work."

GROSS **MOTOR**

"Therapy is fun!"

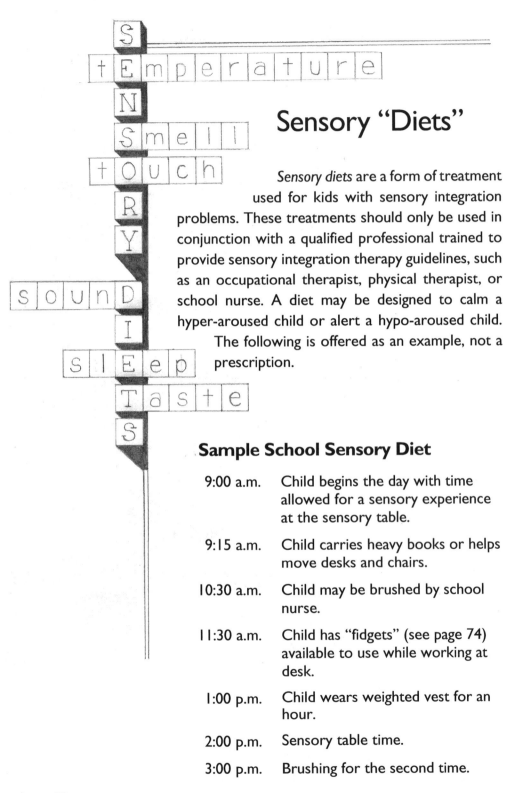

Sensory "Diets"

Sensory diets are a form of treatment used for kids with sensory integration problems. These treatments should only be used in conjunction with a qualified professional trained to provide sensory integration therapy guidelines, such as an occupational therapist, physical therapist, or school nurse. A diet may be designed to calm a hyper-aroused child or alert a hypo-aroused child.

The following is offered as an example, not a prescription.

Sample School Sensory Diet

9:00 a.m.	Child begins the day with time allowed for a sensory experience at the sensory table.
9:15 a.m.	Child carries heavy books or helps move desks and chairs.
10:30 a.m.	Child may be brushed by school nurse.
11:30 a.m.	Child has "fidgets" (see page 74) available to use while working at desk.
1:00 p.m.	Child wears weighted vest for an hour.
2:00 p.m.	Sensory table time.
3:00 p.m.	Brushing for the second time.

Calming and Alerting Activities

Children who easily become over-aroused (hyper-aroused) by sensations can benefit from *calming activities* so that they can focus on the activities, rather than the sensory issue. On the other hand, *alerting activities* may be needed to awaken the hypo-aroused kid. It is important to note that some experiences may alert one child but calm another. Following are some calming and alerting activities for some common school problems.

Calming techniques

If over-aroused to *sound*, try:

- playing soft music in the background
- wearing earplugs/earphones
- humming to block out other sounds
- going to a quiet, "time-out" place to reorganize self, such as under a table or in a safe box in the classroom.

If over-aroused to *touch*, try:

- squeezing or applying deep pressure
- getting a bear hug
- wearing a weighted vest
- being wrapped in a blanket
- being swung in a blanket
- chewing gum
- carrying a heavy book in the classroom
- using "fidgets" (see page 74) at school desk or home
- practicing relaxation skills

- taking a warm bath or shower
- escaping to a "hideout fort" in the classroom/house.

If over-aroused to *smells* or *tastes*, try:

- lavender, vanilla, or banana or other calming smells
- scented stickers, scented play dough, scented markers
- times at a sensory table
- chewing gum
- sucking on hard candy (sugar-free, of course!).

If over-aroused to *sights*, try:

- dimmming lights
- using a "shield" in the play/work area to decrease visual distractions
- wearing tinted glasses
- using colored paper for schoolwork
- visualizing a calm, peaceful scene
- taking a "time-out" from visual stimulation (e.g., going to another room or a special place in the room).

Alerting activities

Alerting activities may be needed to stimulate the hypo-aroused kid. Some examples include:

- doing jumping jacks (star jumps)
- jumping rope
- doing rhythmic movements
- rolling the neck
- doing activities at a sensory table
- using "fidgets" (see page 74) at the table or one's desk
- chewing gum or sucking on hard candy
- sharpening pencils

- erasing the chalkboard
- passing out papers or emptying the trash can for the teacher
- standing at a desk, if desired, or taking movement breaks
- playing with cold water
- listening and/or dancing to loud or fast music
- smelling strong odors, such as perfumes, paints, shaving cream, or scented soaps
- playing tug-of-war
- engaging in outdoor fun, such as climbing, swinging, or spinning.

Other Fun Sensory Ideas

Sensory tables

Sensory tables are a great place for children to have a sensory experience at home or school!! A professional can help you determine the different sensory-eliciting items that will be appropriate for your child. Parents and schools can use large containers to store and rotate the different sensory items. Teachers report a calming and focusing effect when children have an opportunity to use them routinely or as needed. A variety of items with different shapes, colors, and textures may be used. Examples of objects to include in a sensory table are: water, sand, rice, silly putty, beans, koosh balls (like the green one on the front cover), clay, play dough, scented markers, paints, vibrating toys, and blow toys. Different textures, such as sand paper, feathers, terry cloth, felt, and ribbons can add a valuable dimension to the sensory experience.

"Fidgets"

Unlike most items at the sensory table, fidgets are smaller and mobile. Children can have them in their pockets, place them on top of or in their desks at school, or keep them in small containers at the sensory table. Examples of fidgets include the smaller sensory table items, such as koosh balls and silly putty, and other objects such as keys, charms, and water bottles.

Gluten-free scented play dough

By Angela Litzinger

Most play dough contains gluten, which gets under nails and is very difficult to wash off completely when it is time to eat, leading to gluten exposure. If you are looking for a purchased option, Crayola® Model Magic®, and a play dough mix from Miss Roben's Grocery (see the Miss Roben's Grocery website) are currently available and gluten-free (GF).

1 cup GF flour mix (if unable to buy, see "Angela's Kitchen")

½ cup salt

2 teaspoons cream of tartar

1 cup water

1 teaspoon cooking oil

food coloring

Whisk ingredients in a saucepan. Cook over medium heat stirring constantly until mixture thickens and forms a ball. Put play dough on a surface dusted with GF flour mix and, when cooled to a touchable temperature, knead until smooth. While kneading, add in a few drops of scented essential oils until desired intensity is achieved. Suggested scents include almond, cinnamon, citrus, lavender, peppermint, rose, and vanilla. Store in a plastic bag or container after play dough completely cools.

See www.angelaskitchen.com for further information.

Certificate of Achievement

is hereby declared

SENSORY SMART

by Using the Four Sensory Smart Keys

1 — Learn and Teach

2 — Work Hard

3 — Tell Problems

4 — Be Alert and Plan Ahead

Sensational!

Christian
PRESIDENT

CHILD

PARENT / PROFESSIONAL

Helpful Resources

ASK ME about Asperger's Syndrome (video) (2000) London: Jessica Kingsley Publishers.

Berger, D.S. (2000) *Music Therapy, Sensory Integration and the Autistic Child*. London: Jessica Kingsley Publishers.

Bogdashina, O. (2003) *Sensory Perceptual Issues in Autism and Asperger Syndrome: Different Sensory Experiences – Different Perceptual Worlds*. London: Jessica Kingsley Publishers.

Chara, K.A. and Chara, P.J., Jr. (2004) *Allergy Busters: A Story for Children with Autism or Related Spectrum Disorders Struggling with Allergies*. London: Jessica Kingsley Publishers.

Clements, J. and Zarkowska, E. (2000) *Behavioural Concerns and Autistic Spectrum Disorders: Explanations and Strategies for Change*. London: Jessica Kingsley Publishers.

Gutstein, S.F. and Sheely, R.K. (2002) *Relationship Development Intervention with Young Children: Social and Emotional Development Activities for Asperger Syndrome, Autism, PDD and NLD*. London: Jessica Kingsley Publishers.

Jackson, J. (2003) *Multicoloured Mayhem: Parenting the Many Shades of Adolescence, Autism, Asperger Syndrome and AD/HD*. London: Jessica Kingsley Publishers.

Kranowitz, C.S. (1998) *The Out of Sync Child: Recognizing and Coping with Sensory Integration Dysfunction*. New York: The Berkley Publishing Group or www.out-of-sync-child.com

Myles, B.S., Cook, K.T., Miller, N.E., Rinner, L., and Robbins, L.A. (2000) *Asperger Syndrome and Sensory Issues: Practical Solutions for Making Sense of the World*. Kansas: Shawnee Mission. In USA, Autism Asperger Publishing Co.; Outside USA, London: Jessica Kingsley Publishers.Ogaz, N. (2003) *Wishing On the Midnight Star: My Asperger Brother*. London: Jessica Kingsley Publishers.

Overton, J. (2003) *Snapshots of Autism: A Family Album*. London: Jessica Kingsley Publishers.

Quinn, B. and Malone, A. (2000) *Pervasive Developmental Disorder: An Altered Perspective*. London: Jessica Kingsley Publishers.

Sensory Integration International (1986) *A Parent's Guide to Understanding Sensory Integration*. Torrance, CA: Sensory Integration International.

Helpful Organizations

A.D.D. Warehouse
(product catalog for developmental disorders)
1-800-223-9273
www.addwarehouse.com

American Occupational Therapy Association
1-800-668-8255
www.aota.org

American Physical Therapy Association
703-684-2782 or 1-800-955-9848
www.apta.org

American Speech-Language-Hearing Association
1-800-638-TALK
www.asha.org

Association for The Neurologically Disabled of Canada (AND)
www.and.ca

Attention Deficit Disorder Association
1-800-487-2282
www.add.org.

Autism Society of America (ASA)
1-800-329-0899
www.autism-society.org

Geneva Center for Autism
416-322-7877
www.autism.net

Handwriting without Tears
(excellent resource)
301-263-2700
www.hwtears.com

Learning Disabilities Association of America
412-341-1515
www.ldaamerica.org

National Autistic Society (London)
+44(0) 20 7833 2299
www.nas.org.uk

Parents Active for Vision Education (PAVE)
(information on vision problems, which frequently occur with sensory integration problems)
1-800-728-3988
www.pavevision.org

Sensory Integration International (SII)
310-320-9986
www.sensoryint.com

Sensory Resources
www.sensoryresources.com

Therapy Works, Inc
(list of numerous helpful products)
505-897-3478
www.alertprogram.com

United Cerebral Palsy Associations, Inc
1-800-872-5827
www.ucpa.org